Mary's Favorite '30s Quilts
by Mary Koval

Chitra
Publications

Your Best Value in Quilting
www.QuiltTownUSA.com
(800)628-8244

Chitra Publications
2 Public Avenue
Montrose, Pennsylvania 18801-1220

First Printing: 2004

Library of Congress Cataloging-in-Publication Data
Koval, Mary.
  Mary's favorite '30s quilts / by Mary Koval.
    p. cm.
  ISBN 1-885588-56-9
  1. Patchwork—Patterns. 2. Appliqué—Patterns.
3. Quilting. I. Title: Mary's favorite thirties quilts.
II. Title.
  TT835.K682 2004
  746.46'041—dc22
                        2004000528

Edited by................................Debra Feece
Design....................................Diane Albeck-Grick
Illustrations.............................Brenda Pytlik
Photography............................Van Zandbergen Photography,
                        Brackney, Pennsylvania

Our Mission Statement:
We publish quality quilting magazines and
books that recognize, promote, and inspire
self-expression. We are dedicated to serving our
customers with respect, kindness, and efficiency.
www.QuiltTownUSA.com

Introduction

A s children most of us were fortunate enough to have a special person who always made us smile and feel happy. As a child, I had my father's mother—my Grandma Buddy. (Although she passed away when I was 21, she still makes me smile today.) To express my love for her, I am sharing patterns of quilts made during the 1930s and '40s. Traditional patterns such as Grandmother's Fan, Sunbonnet Sue, and Drunkard's Path remind me not only of the quilts she made, but also of her and all grandmothers. In short, all of the quilt patterns in this book summon memories from my childhood.

"Grandma Buddy" was born in 1905 in Kansas City, Missouri, as Lydia Minnie Mary Buddymeyer. Named after her, I grew up in California while she lived in Cedar Springs, Michigan. Every year, my mom, dad, two brothers, sister, and I would jump in the car and drive to Grandma's house. Whether we went there during the summer or during the winter for Thanksgiving or Christmas, my adventurous father took us down many a side road, enabling us to see the country and have great memories of our trips to Grandma's.

As you make these quilts, I hope you think of those people in your life who have made you feel special. You'll only need a little time and a few supplies to open your mind and heart to the endless creative possibilities. Every quilt we make becomes associated with memories—whether they be about the fabrics we use, the events in our lives, or the person for whom we are making it. Make these quilts and create some wonderful memories.

My best,

Mary

Dedication

I dedicate this book to my family: my husband Joe and children Paul, Vicki, and Mary as well as my granddaughter Courtney and my father Roy Stout. Of course, I'd also like to dedicate this book to my Grandma Buddy and to grandmas everywhere.

Contents

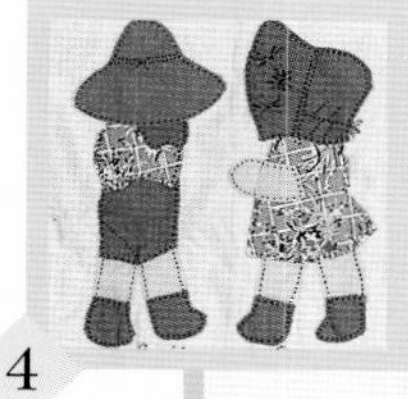

4

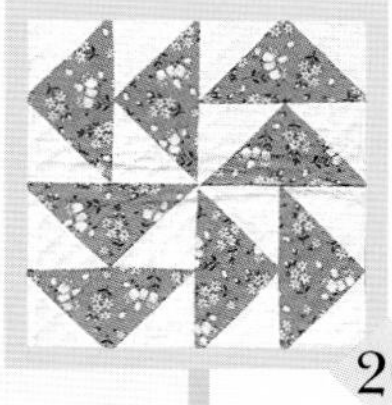

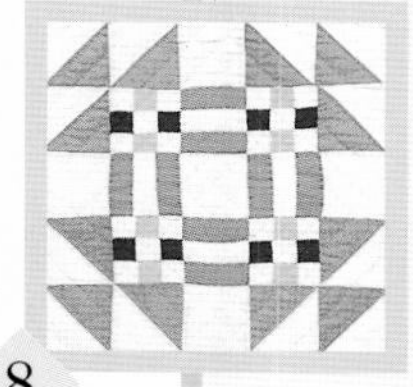

8

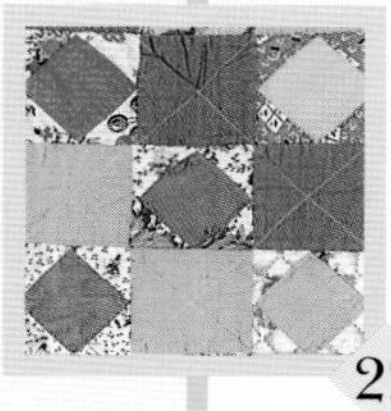

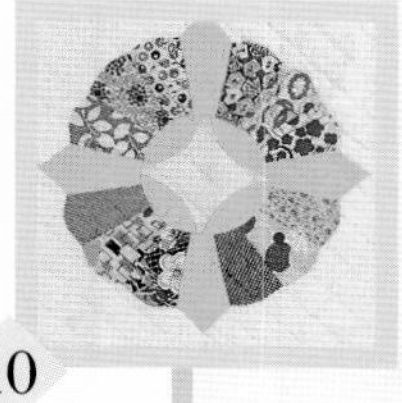

10

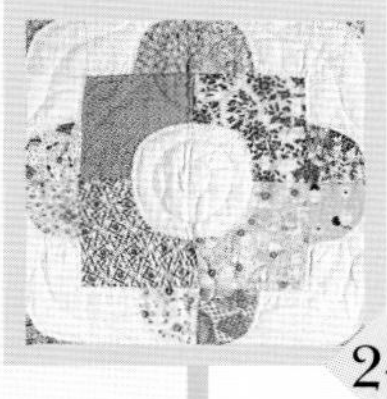

12

14

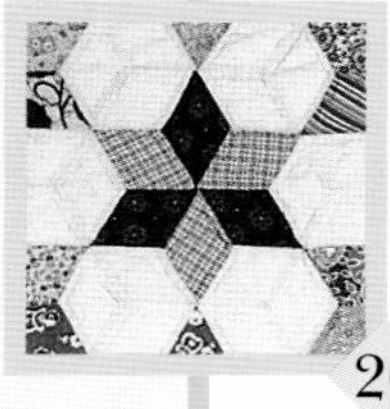

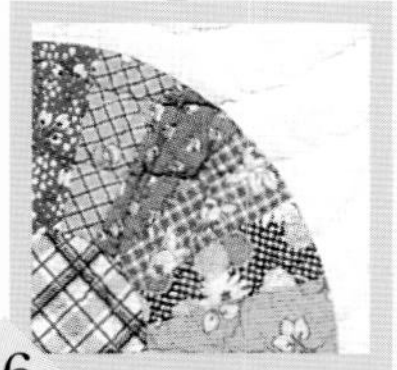

16

20

22

24

26

28

Thank You

To Baum Textile Mills for supplying Mary Koval's line of fabrics, Vintage Storybook: Circa 1930's, which are used in the layouts throughout this book.

Sunbonnet Kids

Quilt Size: 80 1/2" square • ***Block Size:*** 13" square

*Sunbonnet Sue and Overall Sam stand sweetly side-by-side in
"Sunbonnet Kids." Notice the hand-embroidered names beneath them.
Could this have been a friendship quilt?*

Materials

- 4 3/4 yards white
- 4 yards pink
- 1/2 yard peach or beige for the legs and arms
- Assorted bright solids, each at least 9" square
- Assorted bright prints, each at least 5" x 9"
- 7 1/4 yards backing fabric
- 85" square of batting
- Black embroidery floss for the outlines and other assorted colors for the flowers on the hats

Cutting

The appliqué patterns (pages 6 & 7) are full size and do not include a seam allowance. Make a template from each pattern. Trace around the templates on the right side of the fabric and add a 1/4" turn-under allowance when cutting the pieces out. All other dimensions include a 1/4" seam allowance. Cut lengthwise strips before cutting other pieces from the same fabric.

For each of 16 blocks:

- Cut 1 each: girl's dress and boy's shirt, one print
- Cut 1 each: girl's hat, boy's shorts, and bow tie, one solid
- Cut 2 shoes and 2 reversed shoes, same solid
- Cut 1: boy's hat, second solid
- Cut 4 legs and 1 arm, peach or beige

Also:

- Cut 8: 2" x 112" lengthwise strips, white, then cut each of them in half to yield two 56" lengths. You will use 15.
- Cut 16: 14" squares, white
- Cut 12: 2" x 112" lengthwise strips, pink, then cut each of them in half to yield two 56" lengths.
- Cut 4: 3 1/2" x 83" lengthwise strips, pink, for the border
- Cut 9: 2 1/2" x 40" strips, pink, for the binding

Directions

For each block:

1. Referring to the photo, pin the pieces for one block on a 14" white square. Keep all pieces at least 1" from the edges of the square.
2. Appliqué the pieces for the girl in the following order: legs, dress, hat, arm, and shoes.
3. Appliqué the pieces for the boy in this order: legs, shorts, shirt, bow tie, hat, and shoes.
4. Using 3 strands of black embroidery floss, stitch a running stitch around the edge of each piece. Stitch the bow tie, shorts, and hat details in the same manner.
5. Embellish the girl's hat with lazy daisy flowers and French knots.
6. If you wish, embroider a name under each figure as the quiltmaker did.
7. Press the block on the wrong side. Trim the block to 13 1/2" square, keeping the appliqué centered. Make 16 blocks.

For the sashing:

1. Sew two 2" x 56" pink strips to a 2" x 56" white strip to make a panel. Make 11. Set one panel aside.
2. Cut four 13 1/2" sections from each of ten panels, as shown, for a total of 40 sashing units.

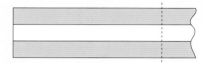

3. Cut twenty-five 2" sections from the remaining panel, as shown.

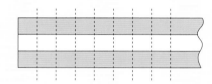

4. Sew two 2" x 56" white strips to a 2" x 56" pink strip to make a panel. Make 2.
5. Cut twenty-five 2" sections from each panel.
6. Sew three 2" sections together to make a Nine Patch, as shown. Make 25.

Assembly

1. Sew 5 Nine Patches and 4 sashing units together alternately to make a sashing strip. Make 5.
2. Lay out the blocks in 4 rows of 4 with the sashing strips between the rows. Place the remaining sashing units between the blocks in each row and on each end.

(continued on page 6)

Sunbonnet Kids

(continued from page 5)

3. Sew the blocks and sashing units together to make 4 rows.

4. Join the rows and sashing strips.

5. Measure the length of the quilt. Trim two 3 1/2" x 83" pink strips to that measurement. Sew them to the sides of the quilt.

6. Measure the width of the quilt, including the borders. Trim the remaining 3 1/2" x 83" pink strips to that measurement. Sew them to the top and bottom of the quilt.

7. Finish the quilt as described in the *General Directions,* using the 2 1/2" x 40" pink strips for the binding. ❤

Full-Size Patterns for Sunbonnet Kids

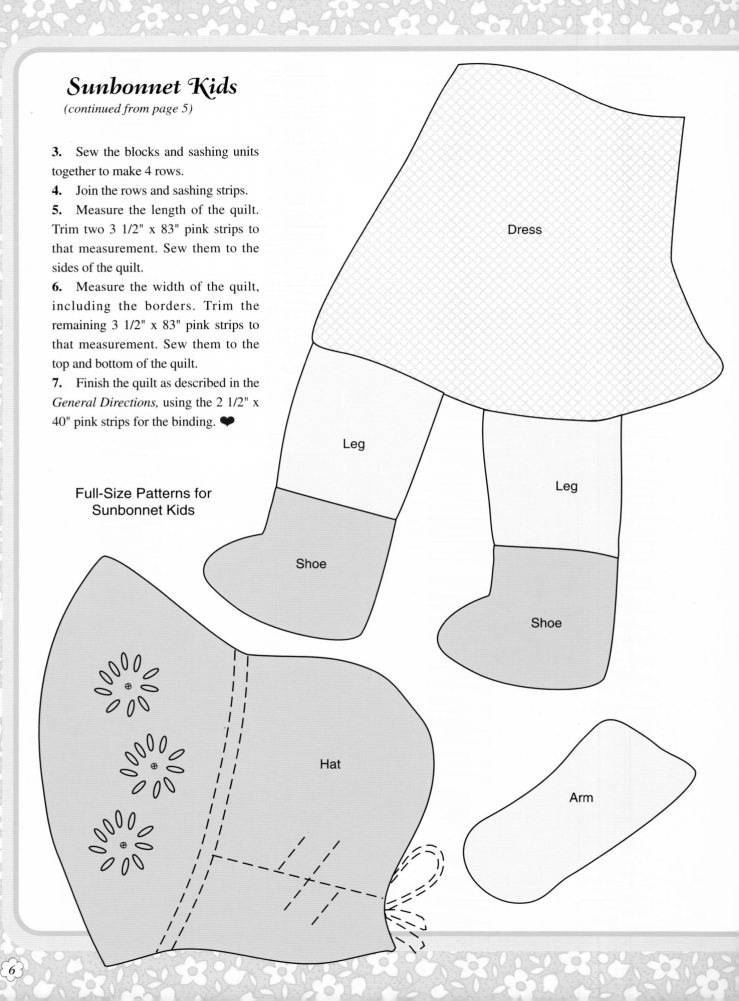

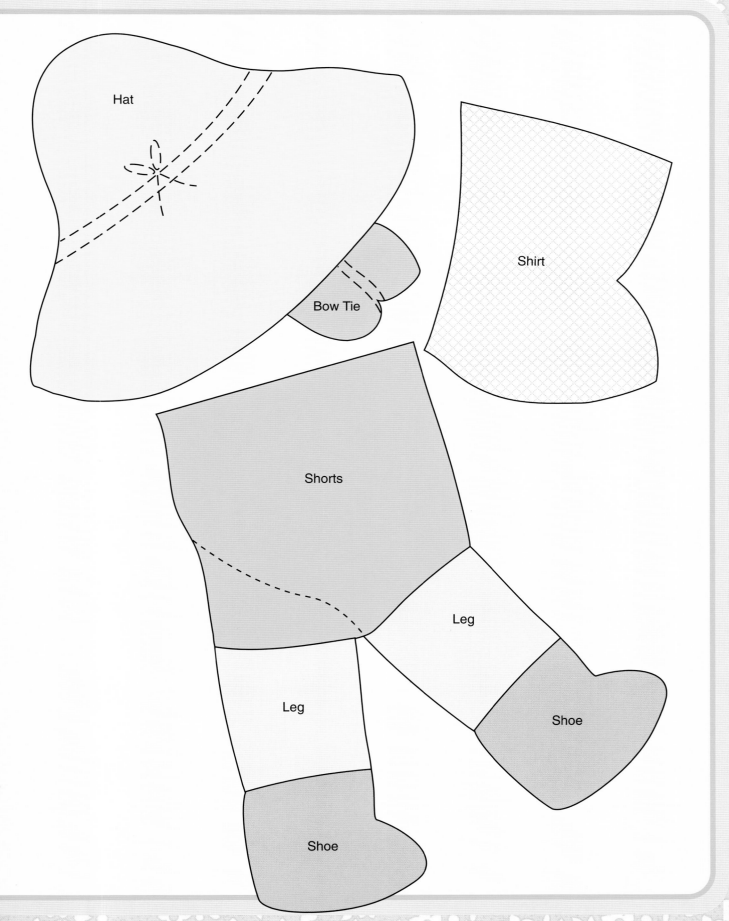

Hat

Shirt

Bow Tie

Shorts

Leg

Leg

Shoe

Shoe

Goose in the Pond

Quilt Size: 87" square • ***Block Size:*** 13 1/8" square

Bright solids give "Goose in the Pond" its simple uncluttered look.
This cheerful quilt could brighten anyone's mood!

Materials

- 5 3/4 yards white
- 3 yards pink
- 3/4 yard green
- 3/8 yard blue
- 3/8 yard yellow
- 7 3/4 yards backing fabric
- 91" square of batting

Cutting

Dimensions include a 1/4" seam allowance. Cut lengthwise strips before cutting other pieces from the same yardage.

For the blocks:

- Cut 19: 1 3/8" x 40" strips, white
- Cut 24: 7" squares, white
- Cut 80: 3 1/8" squares, white
- Cut 24: 7" squares, pink
- Cut 12: 1 3/8" x 40" strips, green
- Cut 6: 1 3/8" x 40" strips, blue
- Cut 5: 1 3/8" x 40" strips, yellow

Also:

- Cut 4: 7 1/4" x 76" lengthwise strips, white
- Cut 24: 5 3/4" x 13 5/8" strips, white
- Cut 4: 3 1/4" x 76" lengthwise strips, pink
- Cut 2 1/2"-wide bias strips, pink, to total at least 360" when joined for the binding
- Cut 4: 7 1/4" squares, pink
- Cut 9: 5 3/4" squares, pink

Directions

1. Draw diagonal lines from corner to corner on the wrong side of each 7" white square. Draw horizontal and vertical lines through the centers.

2. Place a marked square on a 7" pink square, right sides together. Sew 1/4" away from the diagonal lines on both sides. Make 24.

3. Cut the squares on the drawn lines to yield 192 pieced squares. Press the seam allowances toward the pink.

4. Sew two 1 3/8" x 40" green strips to a 1 3/8" x 40" white strip to make a pieced panel. Make 6. Press the seam allowances toward the green.

5. Cut sixty-four 3 1/8" sections from the panels.

6. Sew two 1 3/8" x 40" white strips to a 1 3/8" x 40" yellow strip to make a pieced panel. Make 5. Press the seam allowances toward the yellow.

7. Cut one hundred twenty-eight 1 3/8" sections from the pieced panels.

8. Sew two 1 3/8" x 40" blue strips to a 1 3/8" x 40" white strip to make a pieced panel. Make 3. Press the seam allowances toward the blue. Cut sixty-four 1 3/8" sections from the panels.

9. Sew two yellow sections to a blue section to make a Nine Patch. Make 64.

10. Sew 12 pieced squares, five 3 1/8" white squares, 4 Nine Patches, and 4 green sections into 5 rows. Join the rows to complete a block. Make 16.

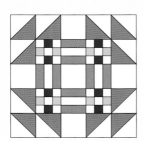

Assembly

1. Sew 4 blocks and three 5 3/4" x 13 5/8" white strips together alternately to make a row. Make 4.

2. Sew four 5 3/4" x 13 5/8" white strips and three 5 3/4" pink squares together alternately to make a sashing row. Make 3.

3. Sew the block rows and sashing rows together.

4. Measure the length of the quilt. Trim 2 of the 3 1/4" x 76" pink strips to that measurement. Sew them to opposite sides of the quilt.

5. Measure the width of the quilt, including the borders. Trim the remaining 3 1/4" x 76" pink strips to that measurement and sew them to the remaining sides of the quilt.

6. Measure the quilt. Trim the 7 1/4" x 76" white strips to that measurement. Sew 2 of them to opposite sides of the quilt.

7. Sew the 7 1/4" pink squares to the ends of the remaining trimmed white strips. Sew them to the remaining sides of the quilt.

8. Fold the quilt in quarters and make a mark on the edge of each border at the center. Using a plate or other round object, mark scallops along the borders, starting from the center mark.

9. Layer, baste, and quilt the quilt, keeping the stitching inside the scalloped lines.

10. Baste around the quilt edge on the marked scallop line. Trim the layers 1/4" beyond the line.

11. Finish the quilt using the 2 1/4" pink bias strips for the binding. ❤

Friendship Circle

Quilt Size: 75" square • **Block Size:** 15" square

Margaret Howard, now 102-years old, of Seward, Pennsylvania, feels yellow brings sunshine into her quilts. And her "Friendship Circle" quilt is as bright today as it was decades ago.

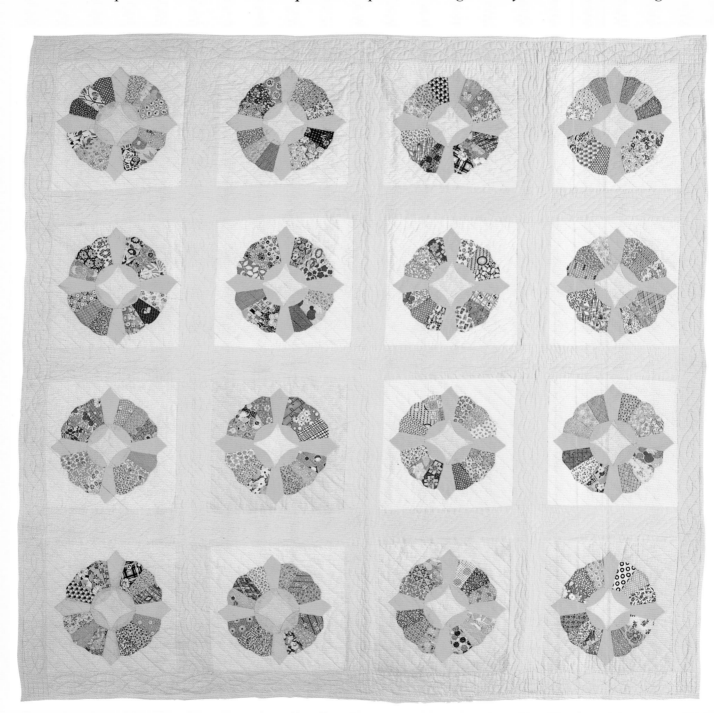

Materials

- 3 3/4 yards muslin
- Assorted prints totaling at least 1 3/4 yards
- 1 1/4 yards dark yellow
- 2 3/4 yards light yellow
- 4 1/2 yards backing fabric
- 79" square of batting

Cutting

Patterns (page 19) are full size and include a 1/4" seam allowance, as do all dimensions given. Make a template from each pattern. Trace around the templates on the right side of the fabric and cut the pieces out on the traced lines. Cut the lengthwise light yellow strips before cutting the binding strips from the same yardage.

- Cut 16: 16" squares, muslin
- Cut 16: A, muslin
- Cut 64: B, dark yellow
- Cut 64: C, dark yellow
- Cut 192: D, assorted prints
- Cut 2: 3 1/2" x 77" lengthwise strips, light yellow
- Cut 5: 3 1/2" x 72" lengthwise strips, light yellow
- Cut 3: 3 1/2" x 63" lengthwise strips, light yellow, then cut four 15 1/2" sections from each strip
- Cut 8: 2 1/2" x 40" strips, light yellow, for the binding

Directions

1. Sew 4 dark yellow B's to a muslin A to make a center unit, as shown.

2. Sew 2 print D's together between the dots, backstitching at each one. Sew a third D to the pair. Make 4.

3. Sew the D sections and 4 dark yellow C's together alternately to make a circle.

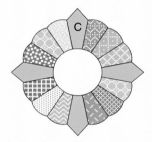

4. Fold a 16" muslin square in quarters. Lightly finger press the folds. Using the folds as a placement guide, pin the center unit to the square, as shown.

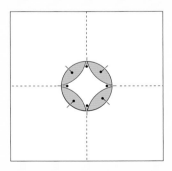

5. Appliqué the pieced circle to the center unit, turning the edge under as you stitch. NOTE: *If you plan to cut the muslin away from the back of the block, stitch just through the center unit and not the muslin square.*

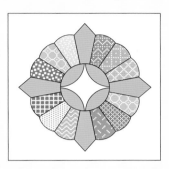

6. Appliqué the outer edge of the pieced circle to the square.

7. If desired, turn the block over and trim the muslin 1/4" inside the appliqué stitches. Press the block on the wrong side.

8. Trim the block to 15 1/2" square, keeping the appliqué centered. Make 16.

Assembly

1. Sew 4 blocks and three 3 1/2" x 15 1/2" light yellow strips together alternately to make a row. Make 4.

2. Measure the rows. Trim the 3 1/2" x 72" light yellow strips to that measurement.

3. Sew the rows and trimmed strips together alternately.

4. Measure the width of the quilt. Trim the 3 1/2" x 77" light yellow strips to that measurement. Sew them to the remaining sides of the quilt.

5. Finish the quilt as described in the *General Directions,* using the 2 1/2" x 40" light yellow strips for the binding. ❤

Flower Wreath

Crib Quilt Size: 40" x 56"

*I purchased "Flower Wreath Crib Quilt" in New York at the same time I bought its
full-size version (page 14). Both quilts were made in the 1930s with reproduction calicoes.*

Materials

- 1 3/4 yards white
- 3/4 yard pink print
- 1 yard green print
- 4" x 6" scrap of yellow print
- 2 1/2 yards backing fabric
- 44" x 60" piece of batting

Cutting

The appliqué patterns (additional pieces on page 18) are full size and do not include a seam allowance. Make a template from each pattern. Trace around the templates on the right side of the fabric and add a 3/16" to 1/4" turn-under allowance when cutting the pieces out. All other dimensions include a 1/4" seam allowance.

- Cut 1: 40" x 56" rectangle, white
- Cut 6: 2 1/2" x 40" strips, pink print, for the binding
- Cut 5: large flowers, pink print
- Cut 10: buds, pink print
- Cut 4: 1" x 8" bias strips, green print
- Cut 1 1/8"-wide bias strips, green print, to total at least 180" when joined for the vine
- Cut 40: large leaves, green print
- Cut 10: small calyxes, green print
- Cut 5: circles, yellow print

Directions

1. Fold the 40" x 56" white rectangle in quarters and crease to mark the center.

2. Measure 6 1/2" out from the center and make marks in an arc to form a circle.

3. Referring to the photo, pin 4 large pink print flowers to the rectangle. Press both long edges of the 1" x 8" green print bias strips 1/4" toward the wrong side. Pin the bias strips to the rectangle, centering the strips on the marks and tucking the ends of the strips under the flowers.

4. Appliqué the strips and flowers.

5. Pin a large pink print flower in the center of the circle. Appliqué it in place.

6. Appliqué a yellow circle in the center of each flower.

7. Pin 20 large green print leaves around the circle. Appliqué them in place.

For the Appliqué border:

1. Sew the 1 1/4"-wide green bias strips together to make a long strip. Press the long edges 1/4" toward the wrong side.

2. Referring to the photo, pin the bias strip to the border of the quilt. Tuck calyxes under the edge of the strip and pin them in place.

3. Tuck buds under the calyxes and appliqué them in place.

4. Appliqué the calyxes, large leaves, and the strip.

5. Finish the quilt as described in the *General Directions,* using the 2 1/2" x 40" pink print strips for the binding. ❤

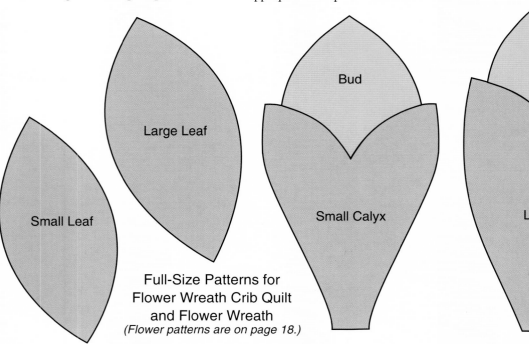
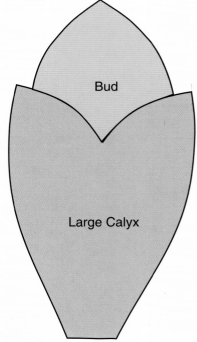

Full-Size Patterns for Flower Wreath Crib Quilt and Flower Wreath
(Flower patterns are on page 18.)

Small Leaf

Large Leaf

Bud

Small Calyx

Bud

Large Calyx

Flower Wreath

Quilt Size: 90" square • **Block Size:** 17" square

*The pink and green calico reproduction fabrics used in the 1930s
to make "Flower Wreath" were copies of 1880s calicoes. The crib-size
accompaniment to this full-size appliqué quilt is on page 12.*

Materials

- 8 yards white
- 2 yards pink print
- 2 1/4 yards green print
- 1/4 yard yellow print
- 8 yards backing fabric
- 94" square of batting

Cutting

The appliqué patterns (pages 13 and 18) are full size and do not include a seam allowance. Make a template from each pattern. Trace around the templates on the right side of the fabric and add a 3/16" to 1/4" turn-under allowance when cutting the pieces out. All other dimensions include a 1/4" seam allowance. Cut lengthwise strips before cutting other pieces from the same yardage.

- Cut 2: 9 1/2" x 74" lengthwise strips, white
- Cut 2: 9 1/2" x 94" lengthwise strips, white
- Cut 2: 25 1/2" squares, white, then cut them in quarters diagonally to yield 8 setting triangles
- Cut 2: 13" squares, white, then cut them in half diagonally to yield 4 corner triangles
- Cut 9: 18" squares, white
- Cut 4: 17 1/2" squares, white
- Cut 6: 2 1/2" x 65" lengthwise strips, pink print, for the binding
- Cut 45: small flowers, pink print
- Cut 20: buds, pink print
- Cut 9: 1" x 32" bias strips, green print
- Cut 1 1/4"-wide bias strips, green print, to total at least 370" when joined for the vine

- Cut 180: small leaves, green print
- Cut 24: large leaves, green print
- Cut 20: large calyxes, green print
- Cut 45: circles, yellow print

Directions

1. Fold an 18" white square in quarters diagonally and crease the folds.

2. Using the creases as guidelines, lightly mark the center of the block. Measure 5 3/4" out from the center and make a mark on each crease. Measuring out from the center, make marks in an arc to form a circle.

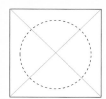

3. Pin a small pink print flower in each corner of the square, using the creases for alignment and overlapping the marked circle.

4. Press both long edges of a 1" x 32" green print bias strip 1/4" toward the wrong side. Cut four 8" lengths from the prepared bias strip and pin them to the square, center-ing the strips on the marked cir-cle and tucking the ends under the flowers.

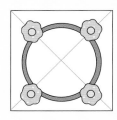

5. Appliqué the strips to the square. Appliqué the flowers.

6. Pin a small pink print flower in the center of the circle. Appliqué it in place.

7. Appliqué a yellow circle in center of each flower.

8. Pin 20 small green print leaves

around the circle. Appliqué them in place. Trim the block to 17 1/2" square, keeping the appliqué centered. Make 9.

Assembly

1. Referring to the Assembly Diagram, lay out the blocks, 17 1/2" white squares, and setting and corner triangles. Sew them into diagonal rows and join the rows.

2. Measure the width of the quilt. Trim the 9 1/2" x 74" white strips to that measurement. Sew them to oppo-site sides of the quilt.

3. Measure the length of the quilt, including the borders. Trim the 9 1/2" x 94" white strips to that measure-ment. Sew them to the remaining sides of the quilt.

4. Appliqué the border as described in "For the Appliqué border" on page 13.

5. Finish the quilt as described in the *General Directions,* using the 2 1/2" x 65" pink print strips for the binding.

Grandmother's Fan

Quilt Size: 67 1/2" x 75" • **Block Size:** 7 1/2" square

Sometimes just a bit of subtle texture is all it takes to bring a simple design that special touch. The alternating dotted prints do just that in "Grandmother's Fan."

Materials

- Assorted bright prints totaling at least 2 1/4 yards
- 1/2 yard green plaid
- 2 1/4 yards light print
- 2 3/4 yards muslin
- 3/4 yard print for the binding
- 4 1/2 yards backing fabric
- 72" x 79" piece of batting

Cutting

Patterns (additional piece on page 18) are full size and include a 1/4" seam allowance, as do all dimensions given. Make a template from each pattern. Trace around the templates on the right side of the fabric and cut the pieces out on the lines.

For each of 45 Fan blocks:

- Cut 6: fan blades, assorted prints

Also:

- Cut 45: quarter circles, green plaid
- Cut 45: background pieces, muslin; or cut 8" squares
- Cut 45: 8" squares, light print
- Cut 8: 2 1/2" x 40" strips, print, for the binding

Directions

1. Sew 2 fan blades together between the dots, backstitching at each one. Make 3.

2. Join the pairs of fan blades in the same manner to make a fan.

3. Sew a green print quarter circle to the small curve of the fan or, if you prefer, appliqué the curved edge of the quarter circle to the fan.

4. Sew the fan to a muslin background piece or appliqué the fan to an 8" muslin square. Make 45.

5. If the fans were appliquéd to muslin squares, trim the muslin behind the fan sections, leaving a 1/4" seam allowance.

Assembly

1. Referring to the photo, lay out the blocks and 8" light print squares in 10 rows of 9.

2. Sew the blocks and squares into rows and join the rows.

3. Finish the quilt as described in the *General Directions,* using the 2 1/2" x 40" print strips for the binding. ♥

Full-Size Patterns for Grandmother's Fan
(Additional pattern is on page 18)

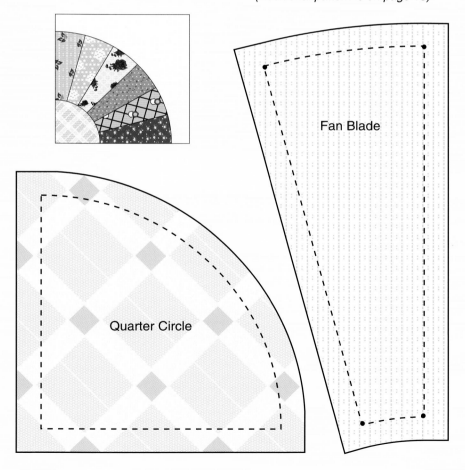

Fan Blade

Quarter Circle

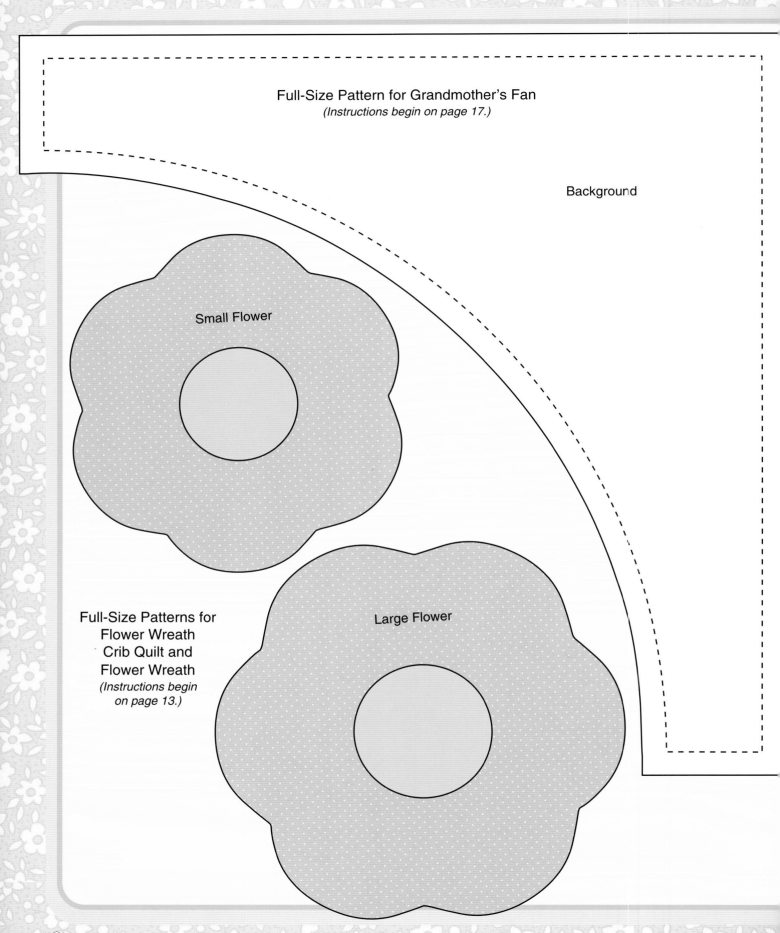

Full-Size Pattern for Grandmother's Fan
(Instructions begin on page 17.)

Background

Small Flower

Large Flower

Full-Size Patterns for
Flower Wreath
Crib Quilt and
Flower Wreath
*(Instructions begin
on page 13.)*

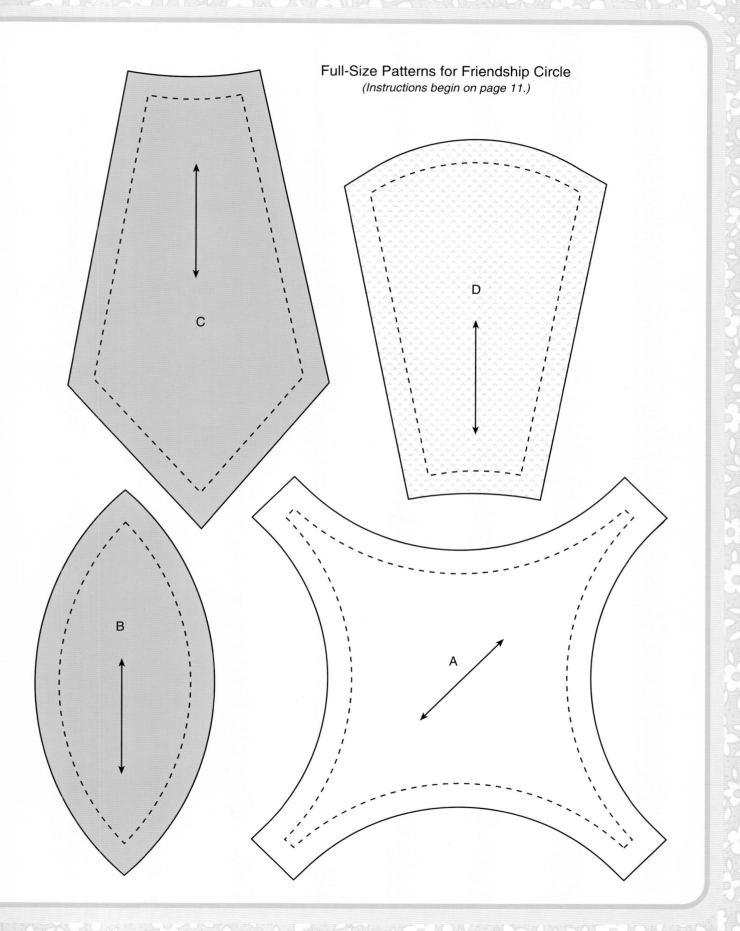

Full-Size Patterns for Friendship Circle
(Instructions begin on page 11.)

Circling Geese

Quilt Size: 83" square • **Block Size:** 12" square

Whenever I see "Circling Geese," I'm tempted to call it an even more playful name—"Pinwheel Goose Chase." That's because I imagine the Pinwheels are set spinning by the geese's flapping wings.

Materials
- 1/4 yard each of 25 prints
- 4 yards white
- 4 yards pink
- 7 1/2 yards backing fabric
- 87" square of batting

Cutting

Dimensions include a 1/4" seam allowance. Cut the lengthwise pink strips before cutting other pieces from the same yardage.

From each print:
- Cut 8: 3 1/2" x 6 1/2" rectangles

Also:
- Cut 400: 3 1/2" squares, white
- Cut 2: 6" x 83 1/2" lengthwise strips, pink
- Cut 2: 6" x 72 1/2" lengthwise strips, pink
- Cut 4: 3 1/2" x 72 1/2" lengthwise strips, pink
- Cut 20: 3 1/2" x 12 1/2" strips, pink
- Cut 9: 2 1/2" x 40" strips, pink, for the binding

Directions

For each of 25 blocks:

1. Draw a diagonal line from corner to corner on the wrong side of sixteen 3 1/2" white squares.

2. Place a marked square on one end of a 3 1/2" x 6 1/2" print rectangle. Sew on the drawn line.

3. Turn the unit wrong side up and press the underneath layers toward the rectangle, as shown. Trim, leaving a 1/4" seam allowance.

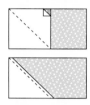

4. Place a marked square on the opposite end of the rectangle. Sew on the drawn line. Press, as before and trim the seam allowance to complete a Flying Geese unit. Make 8.

5. Sew 2 Flying Geese units together to make a quarter block. Make 4.

6. Lay out the quarter blocks, as shown. Sew them into pairs then join the pairs to complete the block. Make 25.

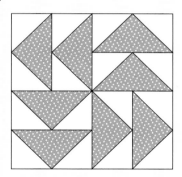

Assembly

1. Join 5 blocks alternately with four 3 1/2" x 12 1/2" pink strips to make a row. Make 5.

2. Join the rows and 3 1/2" x 72 1/2" pink strips alternately.

3. Sew the 6" x 72 1/2" pink strips to opposite sides of the quilt.

4. Sew the 6" x 83 1/2" pink strips to the remaining sides of the quilt.

5. Finish the quilt as described in the *General Directions,* using the 2 1/2" x 40" pink strips for the binding. ♥

Confetti Baby Quilt

Quilt Size: 40" x 55" • ***Block Size:*** 2 1/2" square

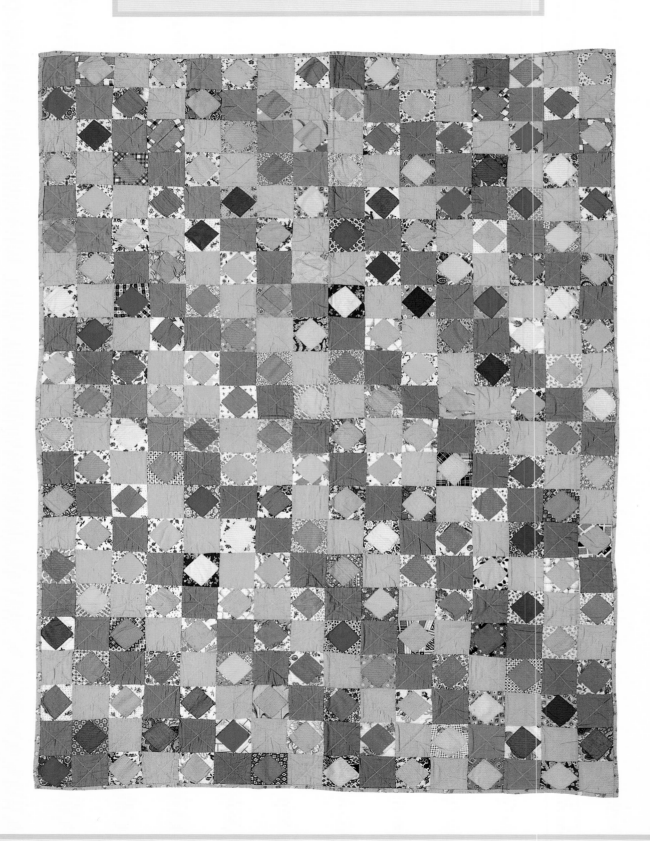

Alternating diagonal rows of pink and blue set off cheerful prints.
There's an overall sense of unity that gives
"Square-in-a-Square Baby Quilt" a dance-like rhythm.

Materials

- 3/4 yard pink
- 3/4 yard blue
- Assorted bright solids totaling one yard
- Assorted light and medium prints totaling 1 1/2 yards
- 5/8 yard pink print for the binding
- 2 3/4 yards backing fabric
- 44" x 59" piece of batting

Cutting

Dimensions include a 1/4" seam allowance.

- Cut 88: 3" squares, pink
- Cut 88: 3" squares, blue
- Cut 176: 2 1/4" squares, assorted bright solids
- Cut 352: 2 1/8" squares, assorted light and medium prints, in matching pairs; then cut the squares in half diagonally to yield 176 sets of 4 triangles
- Cut 6: 2 1/2" x 40" strips, pink print, for the binding

Directions

1. Sew matching print triangles to opposite sides of a 2 1/4" bright square. Press the seam allowance toward the triangles.

2. Repeat for the remaining corners, using matching print triangles, to make a Square-in-a-Square block. Make 176.

3. Lay out 2 Square-in-a-square blocks and two 3" pink squares. Sew them together to make a Four Patch. Make 44.

4. Make 44 Four Patches in the same manner, using the remaining Square-in-a-Square blocks and the 3" blue squares.

Assembly

1. Lay out 2 pink Four Patches and 2 blue Four Patches. Sew them together to make a large block. Make 20.

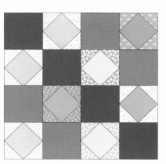

2. Referring to the photo, lay out the large blocks in 5 rows of 4, making pink and blue diagonal chains. Place the remaining Four Patches in a row at the bottom of the layout, maintaining the design.

3. Sew the large blocks into rows. Sew the Four Patches into a row. Join the rows.

4. Finish the quilt as described in the *General Directions,* using the 2 1/2" x 40" pink print strips for the binding.

Drunkard's Path

Quilt Size: 82" square • **Block Size:** 4" square

*The pastel colors of this "Drunkard's Path" make it a classic rendition
of the traditional pattern, which was especially popular during the 1930s.
The unusual shape of its perimeter echoes some of its curved pieces.*

Cutting

Patterns (page 30) are full size and include a 1/4" seam allowance, as do all dimensions given.

- Cut 180: A, assorted prints
- Cut 144: B, assorted prints
- Cut 144: A, white
- Cut 180: B, white
- Cut 2: 5 1/2" x 84" strips, lavender
- Cut 2: 5 1/2" x 74" strips, lavender
- Cut 2 1/2"-wide bias strips, lavender, to total at least 340" when joined, for the binding (If you choose to make your quilt with straight edges, cut the binding strips on the straight of grain.)

Directions

1. Pin a white A to a print B. Sew the pieces together, keeping the edges aligned and easing in the fullness, as shown. Make 144.

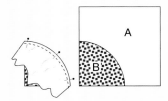

2. Sew a print A to a white B in the same manner. Make 180.

3. Sew 2 white A units and 2 print A units together to make a corner unit. Make 36.

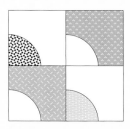

4. Sew 2 white A units and 2 print A units together to make a side unit. Make 36.

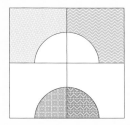

5. Sew 4 print A units together to make a center unit. Make 9.

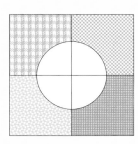

6. Lay out 4 corner units, 4 side units, and a center unit. Sew them into rows and join the rows to make a block. Make 9.

Assembly

1. Lay out the blocks in 3 rows of 3. Sew the blocks into rows and join the rows.

2. Measure the length of the quilt. Trim the 5 1/2" x 74" lavender strips to that measurement. Sew them to opposite sides of the quilt.

3. Measure the width of the quilt, including the borders. Trim the 5 1/2" x 84" lavender strips to that measurement. Sew them to the remaining sides of the quilt.

4. To make the scalloped edges, divide each side of the quilt into quarters and make marks. Draw a gradual curve connecting the marks and corners. Refer to the photo as necessary.

5. Layer, baste, and quilt the quilt as described in the *General Directions,* keeping the quilting inside the drawn lines.

6. Baste around the edge of the quilt just inside the drawn lines. Trim all three layers on the lines.

7. Finish the quilt using the 2 1/2"-wide lavender bias strips for the binding. ♥

Tumbling Block Star

Quilt Size: 80" x 84"

Made with prints widely used in the 1930s and '40s,
"Tumbling Block Star" is a fun pattern that carries right to the binding.

Materials

- Assorted prints totaling at least 4 1/2 yards
- 5 3/4 yards off-white fabric
- 7 1/4 yards backing fabric
- 84" x 88" piece of batting

Cutting

Hand piecing patterns (page 30) are full size and do not include a seam allowance. Make a template from each pattern. Trace around the templates on the wrong side of the fabric and add a 1/4" seam allowance as you cut the pieces out. All other dimensions include a 1/4" seam allowance.

For each of 150 Star units:

- Cut 3: diamonds (A), one print
- Cut 3: diamonds (A), contrasting print

Also:

- Cut 900: diamonds (A), off-white
- Cut 12: B, off-white
- Cut 22: C, off-white
- Cut 2 each: D and DR, off-white
- Cut 9: 2 1/2" x 40" strips, off-white, for the binding

Directions

For each Star unit:

1. Sew a print diamond and a contrasting print diamond together, as shown. Make 3.

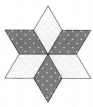

2. Sew the pairs together to make a star.

3. Set 6 off-white diamonds into the star to complete a Star unit. Make 150.

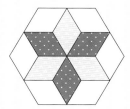

Assembly

1. Referring to the Assembly Diagram, lay out 12 Star units in a vertical row. Sew the units together. Make 7 rows.

2. Lay out 11 Star units and 2 off-white B's in a vertical row. Sew them together to make a row. Make 6.

3. Lay out the 12-Star rows and 11-Star rows alternately.

4. Sew 11 off-white C's to the left-side row and 11 C's to the right-side row.

5. Join the rows. Start by sewing the rows into pairs, then join the pairs.

6. Sew the off-white D's and DR's to the corners of the quilt.

7. Finish the quilt as described in the *General Directions*, using the 2 1/2" x 40" off-white strips for the binding. ❤

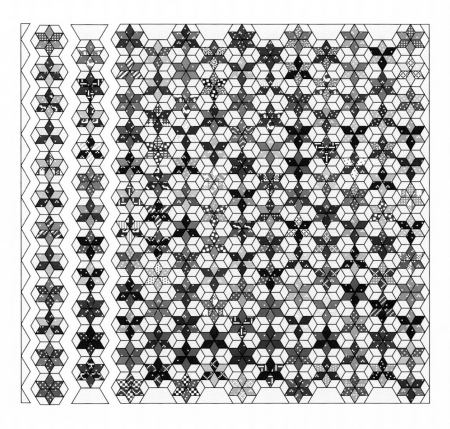

Geo Tiles

Quilt Size: 80 x 108" • **Block Size:** 14" square

"Geo Tiles" has the look of an intricate tile floor. The repetition of the design enables viewers to focus on many different splashes of color.

Materials

- 24 Fat Quarters (18" x 20") assorted prints
- 5 1/4 yards muslin
- 2 1/2 yards blue print
- 7 1/2 yards backing fabric
- 84" x 112" piece of batting

Cutting

Dimensions include a 1/4" seam allowance. Cut the lengthwise muslin strips before cutting other pieces from the same yardage.

For each of 12 blocks:

- Cut 1: 5 1/2" square, one print
- Cut 4: 4" squares, same print
- Cut 2: 2" x 10 1/2" strips, same print
- Cut 2: 2" x 7 1/2" strips, same print

For each of 12 blocks:

- Cut 6: 4 3/8" squares, one print, then cut them in half diagonally to yield 12 triangles

Also:

- Cut 4: 6 1/2" x 86" lengthwise strips, muslin, for the border
- Cut 5: 2 1/2" x 86" lengthwise strips, muslin, for the binding
- Cut 12: 5 1/2" squares, muslin
- Cut 48: 4" squares, muslin
- Cut 24: 2" x 10 1/2" strips, muslin
- Cut 24: 2" x 7 1/2" strips, muslin
- Cut 72: 4 3/8" squares, muslin, then cut them in half diagonally to yield 144 triangles
- Cut 4: 6 1/2" x 86" lengthwise strips, blue print

Directions

1. Sew muslin triangles to opposite sides of a 5 1/2" print square. Press the seam allowances toward the triangles.

2. Sew muslin triangles to the remaining sides to make a center unit. Press, as before.

3. Sew matching 2" x 7 1/2" print strips to opposite sides of the center unit. Sew 2" x 10 1/2" print strips to the remaining sides.

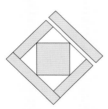

4. Sew 2 muslin triangles to a 4" print square, as shown. Make 4. Press the seam allowances toward the triangles.

5. Sew the pieced triangles to the sides of the center section to complete the block. Make 12.

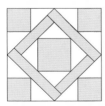

6. Make 12 blocks in the same manner, using the muslin strips, muslin squares, and print triangles.

Assembly

1. Lay out the blocks in 6 rows of 4, alternating light and dark. Sew the blocks into rows and join the rows.

2. Sew a 6 1/2" x 86" blue print strip to a 6 1/2" x 86" muslin strip along their length. Make 4.

3. Measure the length of the quilt. Trim 2 pieced strips to that measurement. Set them aside.

4. Cut four 6 1/2" sections from each of the remaining pieced strips.

5. Sew 2 sections together to make a Four Patch Cornerstone. Make 4.

6. Measure the width of the quilt. Trim the remainders of the pieced strips to that measurement.

7. Sew the Four Patch Cornerstones to the ends of the trimmed strips.

8. Sew the long pieced strips to the sides of the quilt. Sew the strips with cornerstones to the top and bottom of the quilt.

9. Finish the quilt as described in the *General Directions,* using the 2 1/2" x 86" muslin strips for the binding. ♥

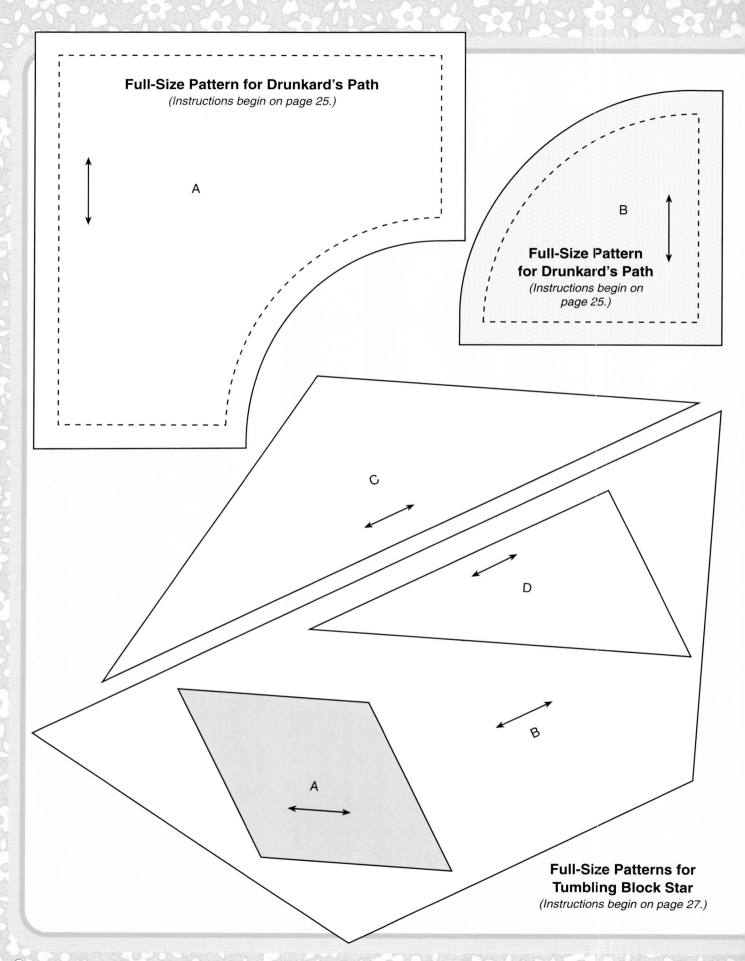

Full-Size Pattern for Drunkard's Path
(Instructions begin on page 25.)

A

B

**Full-Size Pattern
for Drunkard's Path**
*(Instructions begin on
page 25.)*

C

D

B

A

**Full-Size Patterns for
Tumbling Block Star**
(Instructions begin on page 27.)

General Directions

ABOUT THE PATTERNS

Read through the pattern directions before cutting fabric. Yardage requirements are based on fabric with a useable width of 40". Pattern directions are given in step-by-step order. If you are sending your quilt to a professional machine quilter, consult them regarding the necessary batting and backing size for your quilt. Batting and backing dimensions listed in the patterns are for hand quilting.

FABRICS

I suggest using 100% cotton. Wash fabric in warm water with mild detergent. Do not use fabric softener. Dry fabric on a warm-to-hot setting. Press with a hot dry iron to remove any wrinkles.

ROTARY CUTTING

Begin by folding the fabric in half, selvage to selvage. Make sure the selvages are even and the folded edge is smooth. Fold the fabric in half again, bringing the fold and the selvages together, again making sure everything is smooth and flat.

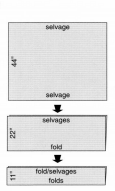

Position the folded fabric on a cutting mat so that the fabric extends to the left for right-handed people, or to the right for left-handed people.

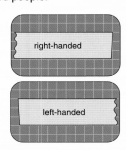

With the ruler resting on the fabric, line up the folded edge of the fabric with a horizontal line on the ruler. Trim the uneven edge with a rotary cutter. Make a clean cut through the fabric, beginning in front of the folds and cutting through to the opposite edge with one clean stroke. Always cut away from yourself—never toward yourself!

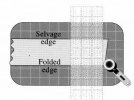

Turn the mat 180°. Move the ruler to the proper width for cutting the first strip and continue cutting until you have the required number of strips. To keep the cut edges even, always move the ruler, not the fabric. Open up one fabric strip and check the spots where there were folds. If the fabric was not evenly lined up or the ruler was incorrectly positioned, there will be a bend at each of the folds in the fabric.

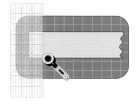

When cutting many strips, check after every three or four strips to make sure the strips are straight.

TEMPLATES

Template patterns are full size and, unless otherwise noted, include a 1/4" seam allowance. The solid line is the cutting line; the dashed line is the stitching line. Place a sheet of firm, clear plastic over the patterns and trace the cutting line and/or stitching line for each one. Templates for machine piecing include a seam allowance, templates for hand piecing generally do not.

MARKING THE FABRIC

Test marking tools for removability before using them. Sharpen pencils often. Align the grainline on the template with the grainline of the fabric. Place a piece of fine sandpaper beneath the fabric to prevent slipping, if desired. For machine piecing, mark the right side of the fabric. For hand piecing, mark the wrong side of the fabric and flip asymmetrical templates before tracing them. Mark and cut just enough pieces to make a sample block, piece it to be sure your templates are accurate.

PIECING

For machine piecing, sew 12 stitches per inch, exactly 1/4" from the edge of the fabric, unless instructed to do otherwise in the pattern. To make accurate piecing easier, mark the throat plate with a piece of tape 1/4" away from the point where the needle pierces the fabric. Start and stop stitching at the cut edges, except for set-in pieces. For set-ins, start and stop at the 1/4" seamline and backstitch.

For hand piecing, begin with a small knot. Make one small backstitch and continue with a small running stitch, backstitching every 3-4 stitches. Stitch directly on the marked line from point to point, not edge to edge. Finish with one or 2 small backstitches before cutting the thread.

APPLIQUÉ

Mark the position of the pieces on the background. If the fabric is light, lay it over the pattern, matching centers and other indicators. Trace lightly. If the fabric is dark, use a light box or other light source to make tracing easier. To hand appliqué, baste or pin appliqué pieces to the background block in stitching order. Use a blindstitch or blanket stitch to appliqué the pieces. Do not turn under or stitch any edges that will be overlapped by other pieces.

Baste pieces (which have been cut on the traced line) in place with a long machine basting stitch or a narrow, open zigzag stitch. Then stitch over the basting with a short, wide satin stitch. Placing a piece of paper between the wrong side of the fabric and the feed dogs of the sewing machine will help stabilize the fabric. Carefully remove excess paper when stitching is complete. You can also turn the edges of appliqué pieces under as for needleturn appliqué, and stitch them in place with a blind-hem stitch.

PRESSING

Press with a dry iron. Press seam allowances toward the darker of the two pieces whenever possible. Otherwise, trim away 1/16" from the darker seam allowance to prevent it from showing through. Press all blocks, sashings, and borders before assembling the quilt top.

FINISHING YOUR QUILT
Marking Quilting Designs

Mark before basting the quilt top together with the batting and backing. Chalk pencils show well on dark fabrics, otherwise use a very hard (#3 or #4) pencil or other marker for this purpose. Test your marker for removability first.

Transfer paper designs by placing fabric over the design and tracing. A light box may be necessary for darker fabrics. Precut plastic stencils that fit the area you wish to quilt may be placed on top of the quilt and traced. Use a ruler to mark straight, even grids. Masking tape can also be used to mark straight lines. Temporary quilting stencils can be made from clear adhesive-backed paper or freezer paper and reused many times. To avoid residue, do not leave tape or adhesive-backed paper on your quilt overnight.

Outline quilting does not require marking. Simply eyeball 1/4" from the seam or stitch "in the ditch" next to the seam. To prevent uneven stitching, try to avoid quilting through seam allowances wherever possible.

Basting

Tape the backing, wrong side up, on a flat surface to anchor it. Smooth the batting on top, followed by the quilt top, right side up. Baste the three layers together. Begin at the center and baste horizontally, then vertically. Add more lines of basting approximately every 6" until the entire top is secured.

Quilting

Quilting is done with a short, strong needle called a "between." The lower the number (size), the larger the needle. Begin with an 8 or 9 and progress to a 10 to 12. Use a thimble on the middle finger of the hand that pushes the needle. Begin quilting at the center of the quilt and work outward to keep the tension even and the quilting smooth.

Using an 18" length of quilting thread knotted at one end, insert the needle through the quilt top only and bring it up exactly where you will begin. Pop the knot through the fabric to bury it. Push the needle straight down into the quilt with the thimbled finger of the upper hand and slightly depress the fabric in front of the needle with the thumb. Redirect the needle back to the top of the quilt using the middle or index finger of the lower hand.

Repeat with each stitch, using a rocking motion. Finish by knotting the thread close to the surface and popping the knot through the fabric to bury it. Remove basting when the quilting is complete.

If you wish to machine quilt, I recommend consulting one of the many fine books available on that subject.

Binding

Cut binding strips with the grain for straight-edge quilts. To make 1/2" finished binding, cut 2 1/2"-wide strips. Sew the strips together with diagonal seams; trim and press seam allowances open.

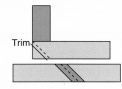

Fold the strip in half lengthwise, wrong side in, and press. Position the strip on the right side of the quilt top, aligning the raw edges of the binding with the edge of the quilt top. Leaving 6" of the binding strip free and beginning a few inches from one corner, stitch the binding

to the quilt with a 1/4" seam allowance measuring from the raw edge of the quilt top. When you reach a corner, stop stitching 1/4" from the edge of the quilt top and backstitch. Clip the threads and remove the quilt from the machine. Fold the binding up and away from the quilt, forming a 45° angle, as shown.

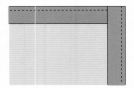

Keeping the angled fold secure, fold the binding back down. This fold should be even with the edge of the quilt top. Begin stitching at the fold.

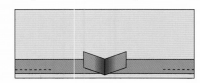

Continue stitching around the quilt in this manner to within 6" of the starting point. To finish, fold both strips back along the edge of the quilt so that the folded edges meet about 3" from both lines of stitching and the binding lies flat on the quilt. Finger press to crease the folds. Measure the width of the folded binding. Cut the strips that distance beyond the folds. (In this case 1 1/4" beyond the folds.)

Open both strips and place the ends at right angles to each other, right sides together. Fold the bulk of the quilt out of your way. Join the strips with a diagonal seam, as shown.

Trim the seam allowance to 1/4" and press it open. Refold the strip, wrong side in. Place the binding flat against the quilt, and finish stitching it to the quilt. Trim excess batting and backing so that the binding edge will be filled with batting when you fold the binding to the back of the quilt. Blindstitch the binding to the back, covering the seamline.

Remove visible markings. Sign and date your quilt.